AF378441

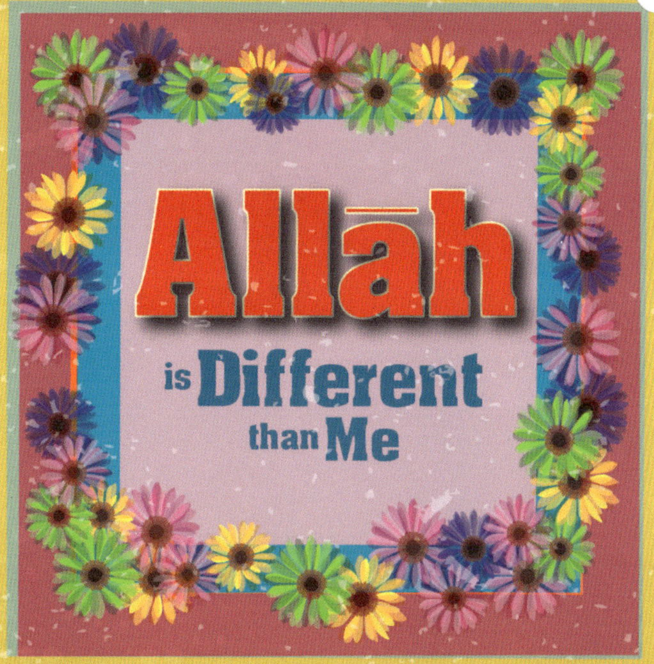

PUBLISHER: GREEN FIG

Green Fig
www.gogreenfig.com

CHY Illustration & Design

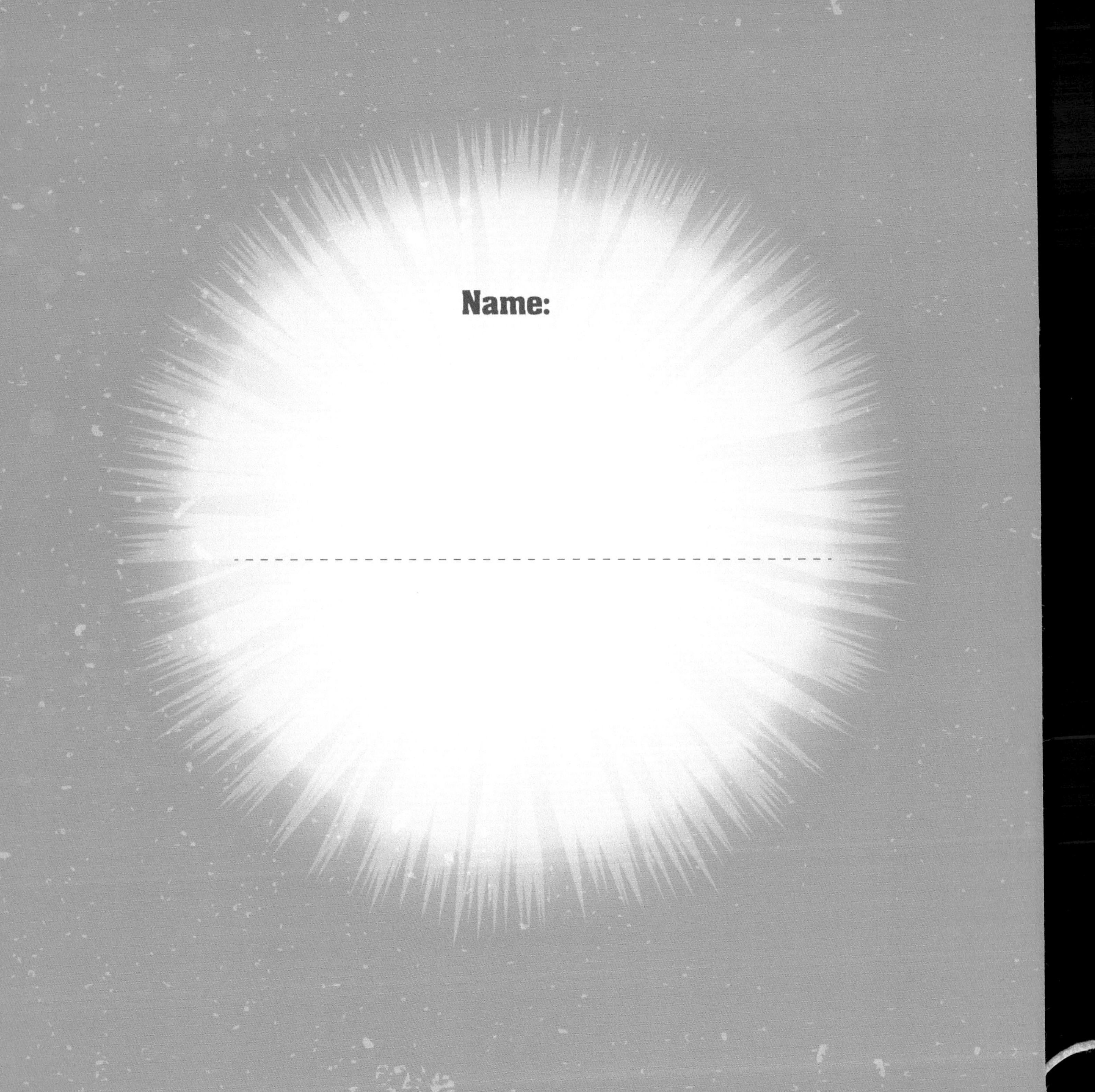
Name:

Note to Parents & Educators

The road to everlasting happiness necessitates the acquisition of Religious Knowledge, the most important of which is that of Tawheed since it relates to knowing God, our Creator. Many parents take great care in feeding their children, dressing them and enrolling them in schools. However, the real fulfillment in parenting is one which cares about the child's Hereafter and strives for their everlasting happiness. To attain this fulfillment, parents must invest in supporting their children's knowledge of Tawheed so they have the proper belief in the oneness of God.

The great scholar and saint Al Junayd Al Baghdadiyy (830-910) defined Tawheed as ``differentiating the Eternal from the created``. To know that God is not similar to the creations is the essence of the science of Tawheed, as mentioned in many verses in the Qur'an. Allah said in Surat النَّحل, verse # 74:

{ فَلاَ تَضرِبوا لِلَّه الأمثال }. This means, ``Do not assign similars or partners to Allah.`` No one is similar to Allah and He is not compared to the creations. His self is not like created selves and His attributes do not resemble created attributes.

Considering the paramount importance of this topic, Green Fig collaborated closely with CHY Illustration & Design to craft the book **Allah is Different than Me**. Its robust content combined with smartly conceptualized and expressive visuals serve to attract the attention of children and promote ease of understanding. The knowledge that children will gain from this book is so precious and will serve as a seed planted in their hearts, growing and blossoming as they become older ان شاء اللَّه.

Green Fig Publishers

Tawheed
is knowing
the **Creator**
is different
from the
creation.

God
is the
Creator.

Everything
else is a
creation.

God
has no
beginning.

Everything
else has a
beginning.

God does not
resemble
anything,

and nothing
resembles
Him.

I am a
creation.

God
created
me.

God

is not like

me.

I am a body
I have organs.

I am composed of parts.
God is not a body. God does not have organs or parts.

I have a form,
a shape,

and a color.

Brown Hair

Blue Eyes

White Pinkish Skin

God does not have a form, a shape or a color.

I have a size

I am bigger than a cat,

but smaller than my dad

I am getting taller
2 years ago
today
God does not have a size.

I have senses.
God is not attributed with senses.
I see with my eyes.
I don't see in the dark
or when my
eyes are closed.

A hawk can see
much better than me.

Even a cat can see
in the dark.

God sees
everything
without an
eye.

I hear with my ears.
I don't hear what is very far from me.
I don't hear when I am asleep.

I even cannot hear all what animals can hear.

God hears everything without an ear.

I smell with my nose.
I smell different odors, some are nice
and some are nasty.

Sometimes I don't smell when I have a bad cold.

God created all the smells and knows about them.

God is not attributed with a sense of smell.

I taste with my tongue.
Some things taste sour,
some sweet

God created all the tastes and knows about them.

God is not attributed with a sense of taste.

I can touch with my hands many things.

My mother skin feels soft.

The tree bark in our backyard feels rough.

God does not touch and cannot be touched.

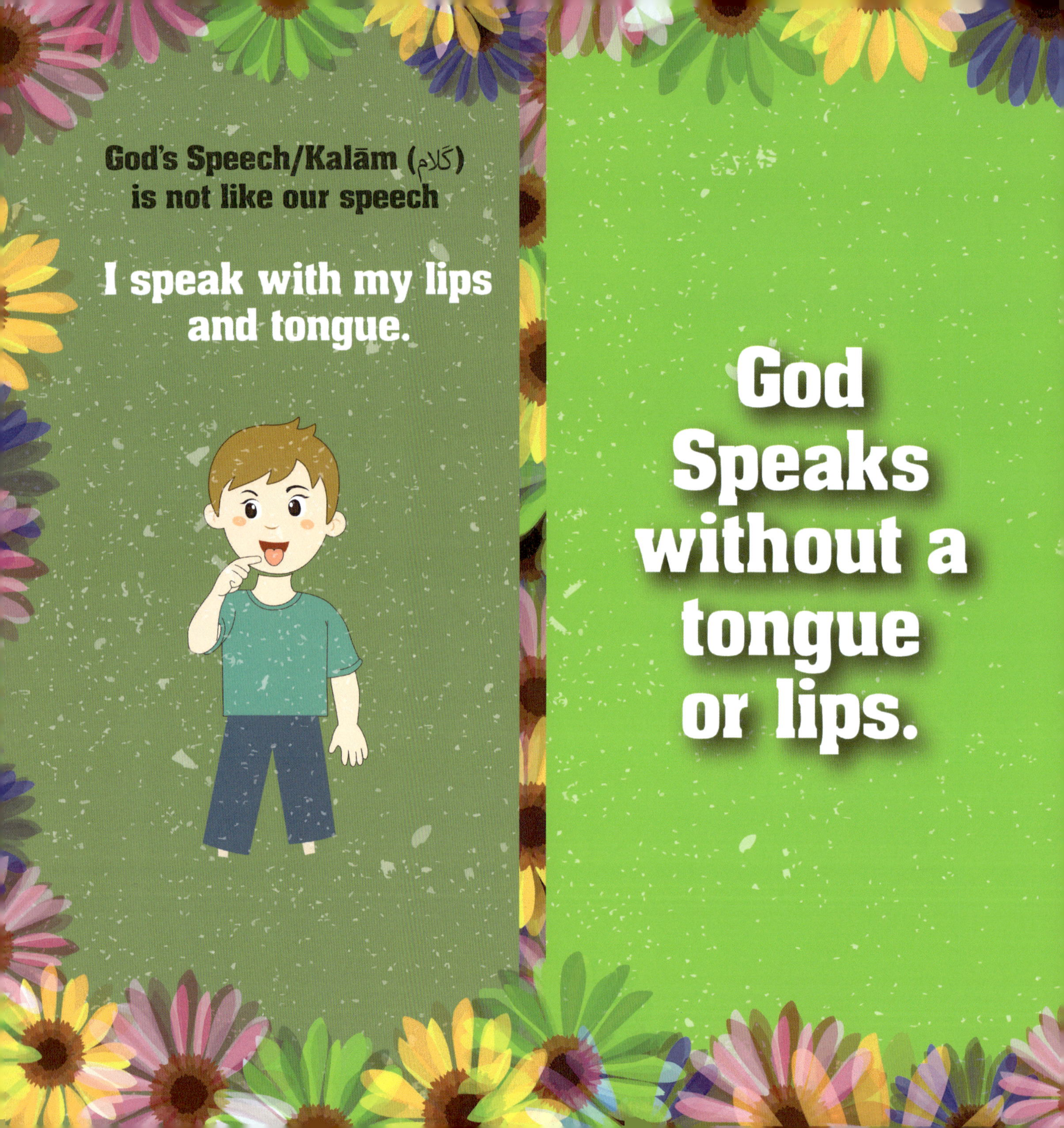

God's Speech/Kalām (کلام)
is not like our speech

I speak with my lips
and tongue.

God
Speaks
without a
tongue
or lips.

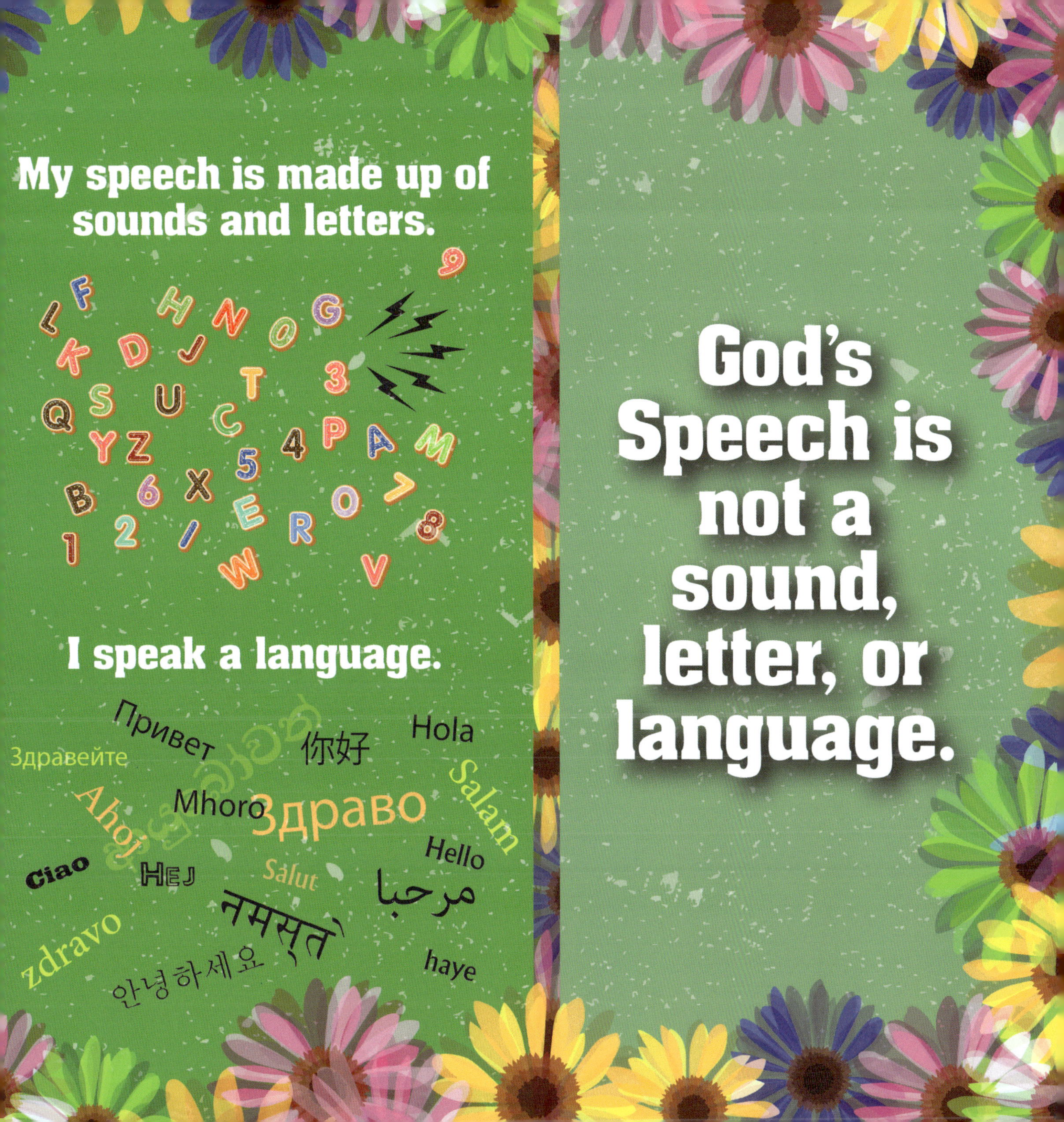

My speech is made up of sounds and letters.

I speak a language.

Привет
你好
Hola
Здравейте
Salam
Ahoj
Mhoro
Здраво
Ciao
Hej
Salut
Hello
नमस्ते
مرحبا
zdravo
안녕하세요
haye

God's Speech is not a sound, letter, or language.

I am in a place.
God is not in a place. God is not on earth, nor in the heavens, nor in any other place.

I move from one place to another
Sometimes I stay still.
God is not attributed with movement or stillness.

I sit.

I have an upper and lower part that bends for me to sit.

I sit on a chair in class

Sometimes I sit on the ground with my friend.

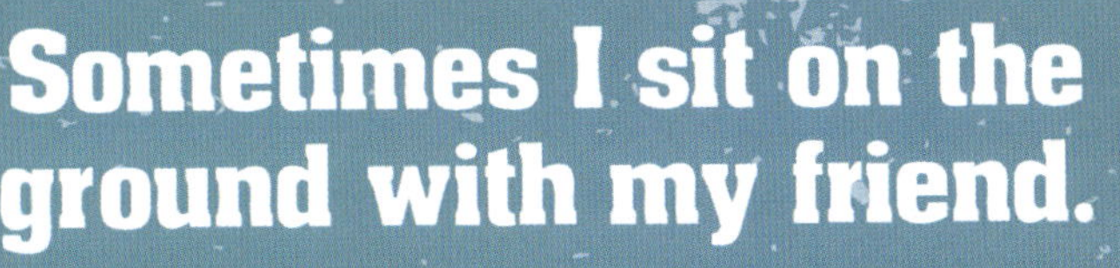

I sit to ride on a bike.

God is not a body. God does not have an upper or lower part that bends.

God is not attributed with sitting.

I have feelings and emotions.
I am happy when I play with my friends.
I miss them when I don't see them for a long time.

Sometimes I am sad.
God is not attributed with feelings and emotions.

I need many things.
I need water and food.

I need to breathe.
I need to rest and sleep.
God does not need anything.

My life is different from God's life

My life is with flesh, blood, and soul.

God's life is not with flesh, blood, or soul.

My life will come
to an end one day.

**God is alive
without an
end.**

I change.
I was not able
to walk when
I was a baby.

I did not have any
teeth either.

My old shirt does not fit me anymore.

God does not change.

I have a family.
I have a mother
and a father.
One day, I might have children.

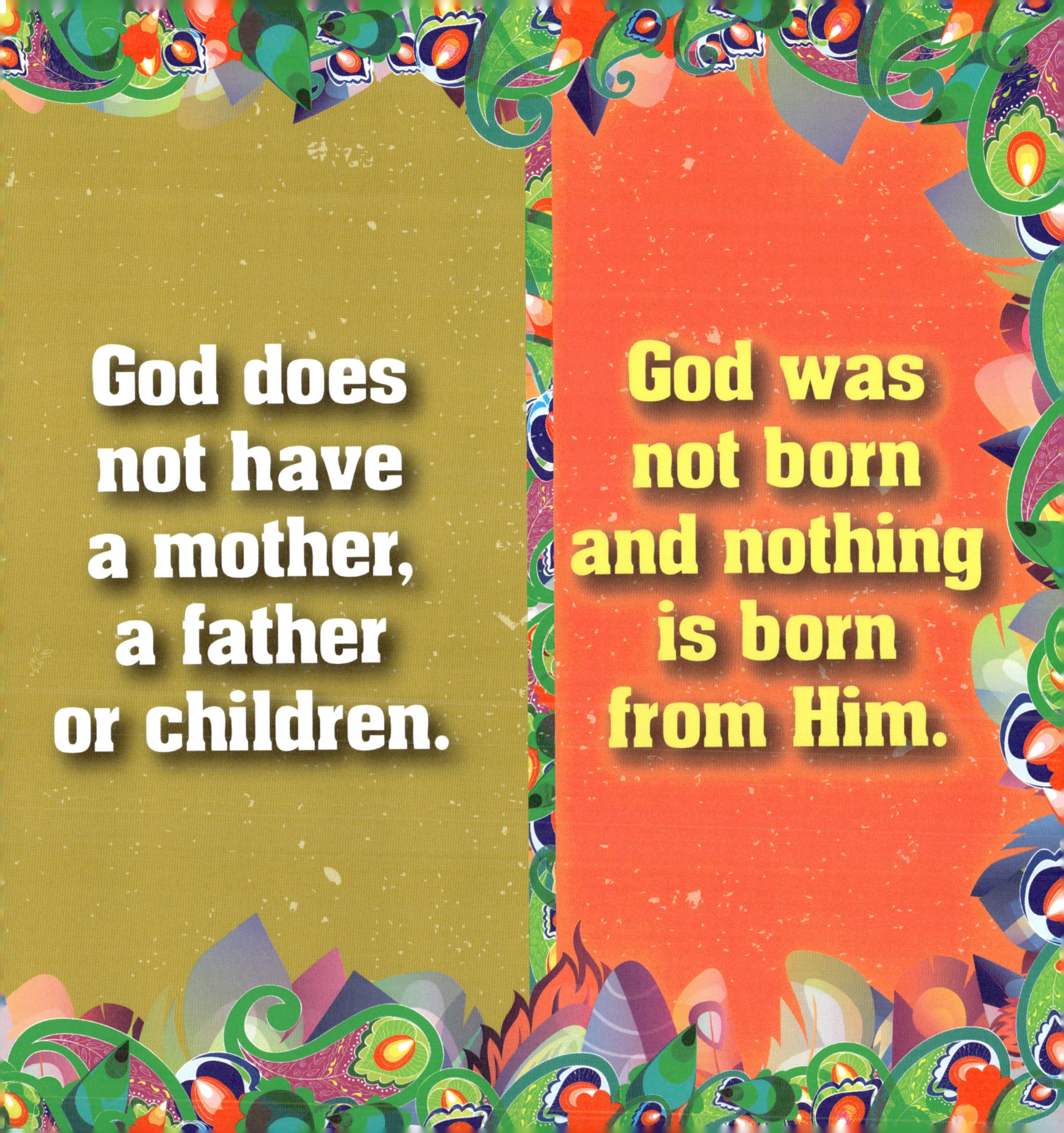

God does
not have
a mother,
a father
or children.

God was
not born
and nothing
is born
from Him.

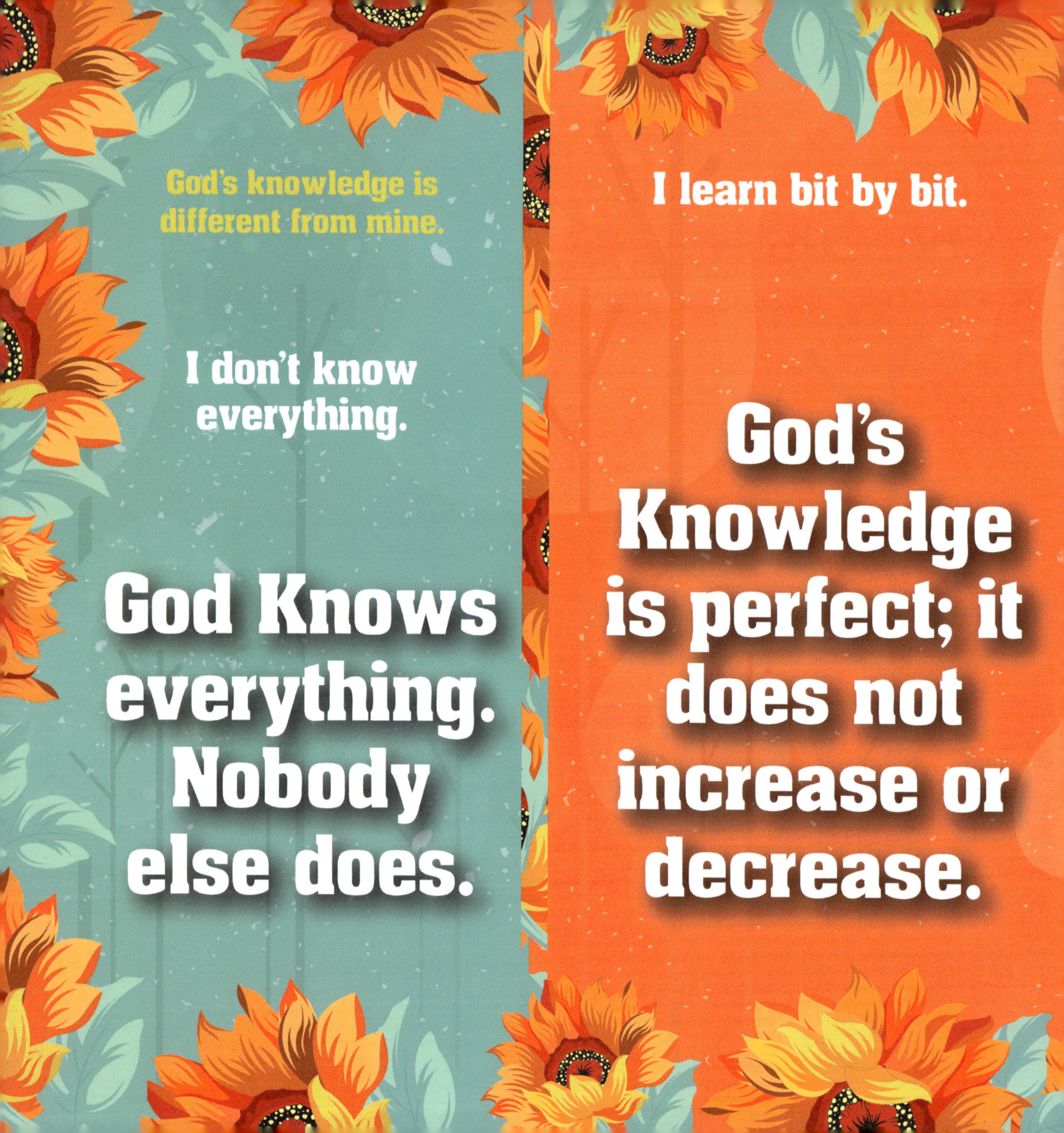

God's knowledge is different from mine.

I don't know everything.

God Knows everything. Nobody else does.

I learn bit by bit.

God's Knowledge is perfect; it does not increase or decrease.

I learn with a teacher.
Sometimes I forget
what I learned

8 × 7 = ??

God knows
everything
without a
teacher.

I can imagine
many things.

I can imagine flying
horses with turquoise
wings.

I can imagine myself
flying on a carpet...

Looking down at trees with golden trunks.

God cannot be imagined. Whatever I imagine is a creation. God is different from whatever I can imagine.

God is different from me and from any other creation.

Tawheed is knowing God is different from the creation.

Encourage your child to memorize

﴿ قُلْ هُوَ اللَّهُ أَحَدٌ ﴾

Which means:

Allāh is one without partners.

﴿ اللَّهُ الصَّمَدُ ﴾

Which means:

Allāh does not need anything and everything needs Allāh.

﴿ لَمْ يَلِدْ وَلَمْ يُولَدْ ﴾

Which means:

Allāh does not have children;
Allāh does not have a mother or a father.

﴿ وَلَمْ يَكُنْ لَهُ كُفُوًا أَحَدٌ ﴾

Which means:

Nothing is similar or equal to Allāh.

The Proud Muslim Kids series by Green Fig is designed to engagingly teach youngsters basic concepts of Islam in a way that speaks to their hearts and minds. Each book in the series is crafted by a staff of qualified educators, writers, illustrators, parents and children. Not only is the Proud Muslim Kids series designed to supplement the early childhood and elementary Islamic curriculum, it is a great addition to any school or home library. Covering a wide variety of topics such as the Five Pillars of Islam, Islamic culture, and Islamic history, parents and children will return to these books and enjoy them together time and time again.